For Helen Flint, teacher, gardener and friend to the butterflies — K.F.

For Granny, Jill — A.P.

Brimming with creative inspiration, how-to projects, and useful information to enrich your everyday life, Quarto Knows is a favourite destination for those pursuing their interests and passions. Visit our site and dig deeper with our books into your area of interest: Quarto Creates, Quarto Cooks, Quarto Homes, Quarto Lives, Quarto Drives, Quarto Explores, Quarto Gifts, or Quarto Kids.

The Butterfly House © 2019 Quarto Publishing plc.
Written by Katy Flint.
Illustrations © 2019 Alice Pattullo.
Natural history consultation by Barbara Taylor.

First Published in 2019 by Frances Lincoln Children's Books, an imprint of The Quarto Group.
The Old Brewery, 6 Blundell Street, London N7 9BH, United Kingdom.
T (0)20 7700 6700 F (0)20 7700 8066 www.QuartoKnows.com

The right of Alice Pattullo to be identified as the illustrator has been asserted by her in accordance with the Copyright, Designs and Patents Act, 1988 (United Kingdom).

All rights reserved.

No part of this publication may be reproduced, stored in a retrieval system, or transmitted, in any form, or by any means, electrical, mechanical, photocopying, recording or otherwise without the prior written permission of the publisher or a licence permitting restricted copying.

A catalogue record for this book is available from the British Library.

ISBN 978-1-78603-974-3

The illustrations were created with brush and Indian ink, collaged hand-painted patterns, and digital composition.
Set in Didot bold, Minik regular and True North script.

Published by Rachel Williams
Designed by Nicola Price
Production by Jenny Cundill and Kate O'Riordan
Manufactured in China in 012019

9 8 7 6 5 4 3 2 1

THE BUTTERFLY HOUSE

Written by Katy Flint

Illustrated by Alice Pattullo

Frances Lincoln
Children's Books

Welcome to the butterfly house!
This house is magical. Its glass walls are wide and its ceilings are never-ending. It contains mountains, rainforests, deserts, meadows, marshes and rivers. These habitats provide a home for many of the major butterfly and moth families in the world.

Butterflies are often thought of as the world's most beautiful insects. There are over 180,000 species of butterflies and moths, with ten times more kinds of moths than butterflies. They make up seven per cent of all life forms on Earth and have been alive since the time of the dinosaurs! They live in every part of the world, except Antarctica. You will meet some of these species as you wander round.

Pay attention to their features and you'll be an expert butterfly spotter in no time!

CHECKLIST

Let's explore! Take your checklist around the house with you, and see which species you can spot on the next pages.

Monarch butterfly

Owl butterfly

Blue morpho

Atlas moth

Luna moth

Christmas light moth caterpillar

THE HATCHERY

Come into this room and see where we hatch all our caterpillars. During their lifetimes, butterflies and moths undergo a complete, four-stage life cycle.

Once a caterpillar has hatched from its egg, it eats and eats. The caterpillar gets bigger and bigger, until it's time to make a pupa. Inside the pupa, the body of the caterpillar is broken down and built into a butterfly. This transformation is called a metamorphosis. Look at the diagram below to see what happens in our warm and cosy hatchery!

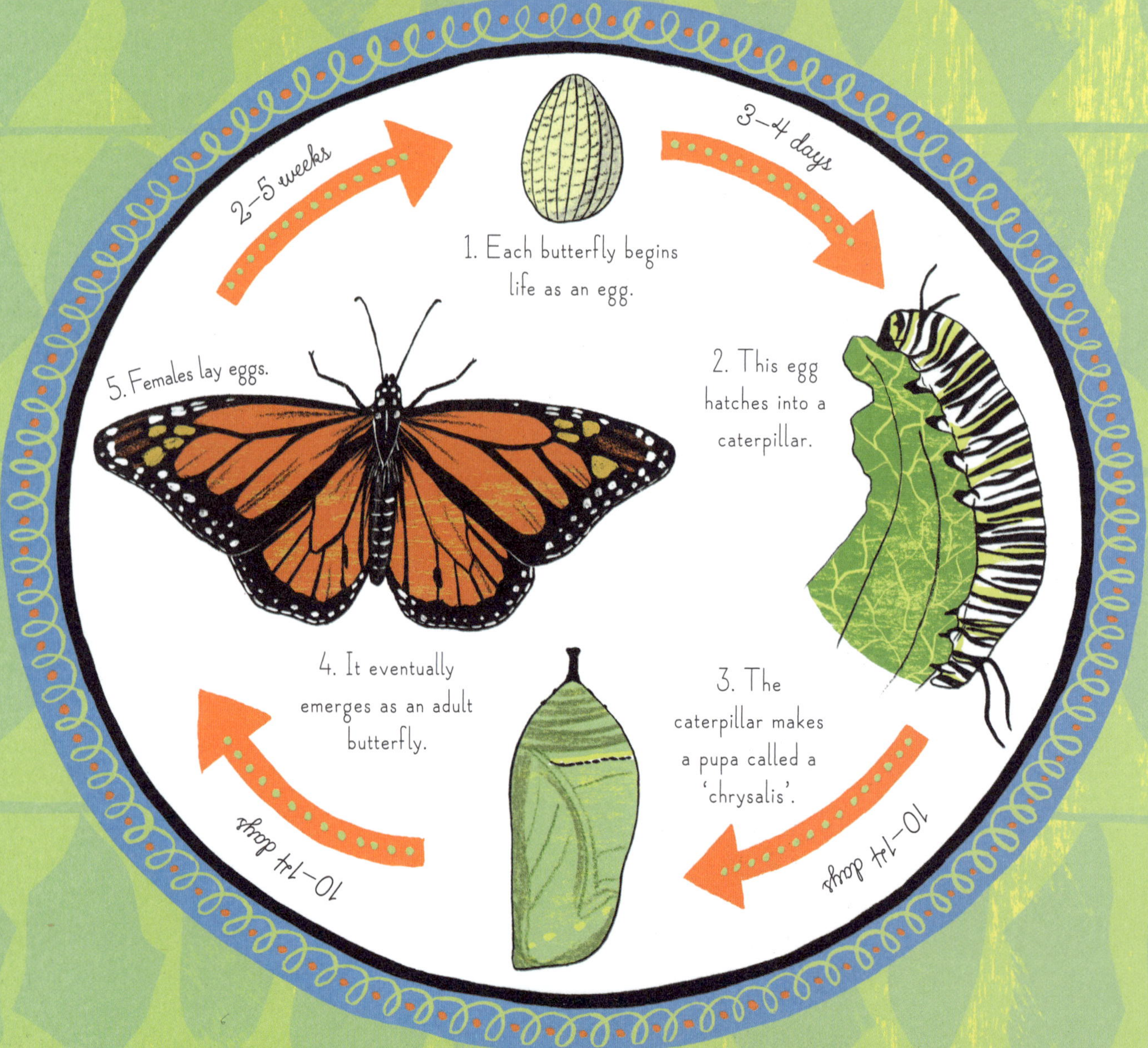

1. Each butterfly begins life as an egg.
2. This egg hatches into a caterpillar.
3. The caterpillar makes a pupa called a 'chrysalis'.
4. It eventually emerges as an adult butterfly.
5. Females lay eggs.

2–5 weeks · 3–4 days · 10–14 days · 10–14 days

Typical life cycle of a monarch butterfly

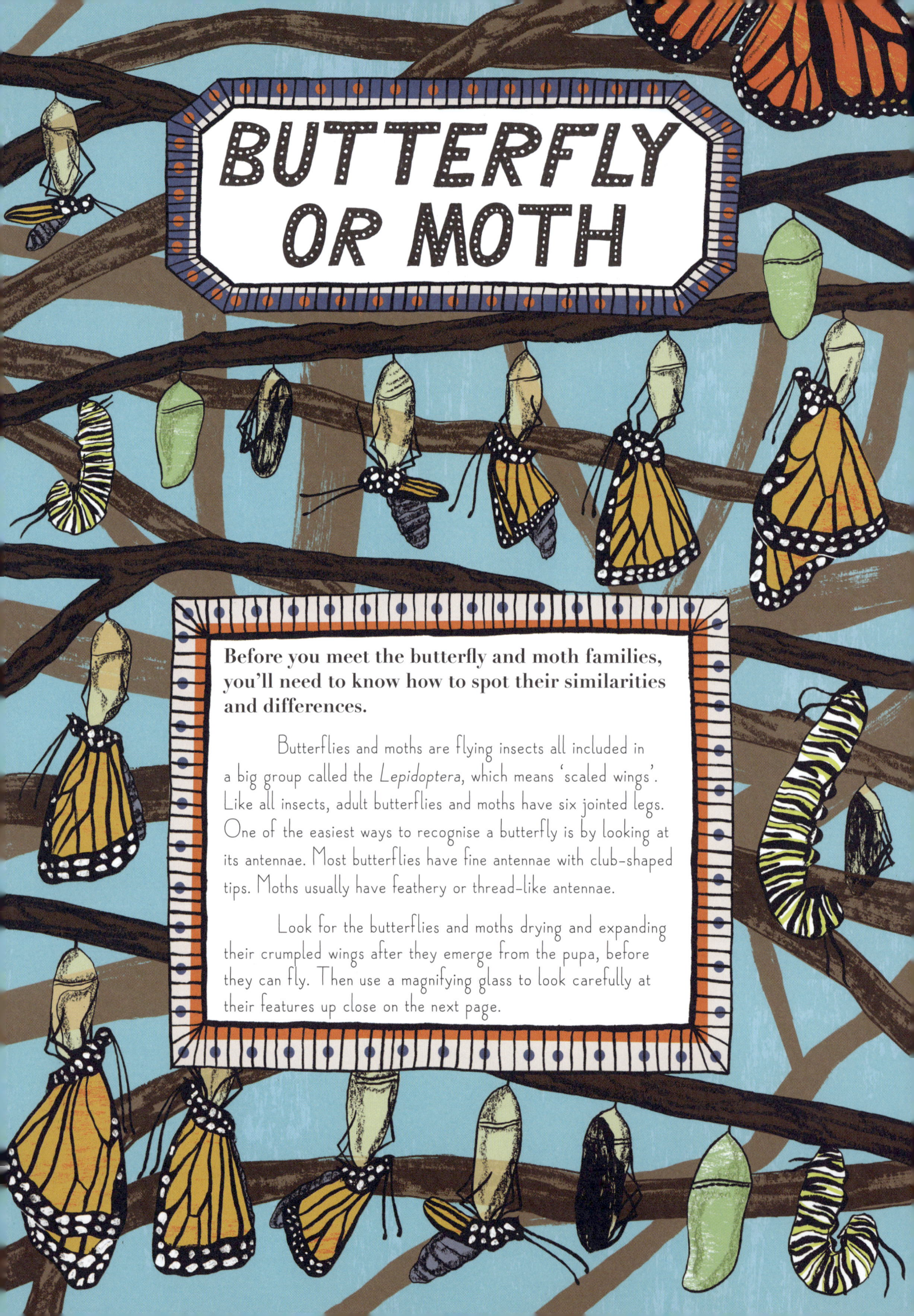

BUTTERFLY OR MOTH

Before you meet the butterfly and moth families, you'll need to know how to spot their similarities and differences.

Butterflies and moths are flying insects all included in a big group called the *Lepidoptera*, which means 'scaled wings'. Like all insects, adult butterflies and moths have six jointed legs. One of the easiest ways to recognise a butterfly is by looking at its antennae. Most butterflies have fine antennae with club-shaped tips. Moths usually have feathery or thread-like antennae.

Look for the butterflies and moths drying and expanding their crumpled wings after they emerge from the pupa, before they can fly. Then use a magnifying glass to look carefully at their features up close on the next page.

Swallowtail butterfly

Most butterflies are active in the daytime.

- Head
- Eyes
- Thin antennae with club-shaped tips
- Legs
- Thorax
- Abdomen
- Veins
- Light-reflecting scales

Most butterflies fold their wings upright when they rest.

Wings move together in flight

Garden tiger moth

Moths can be just as beautiful and colourful as butterflies – as you will see when you explore!

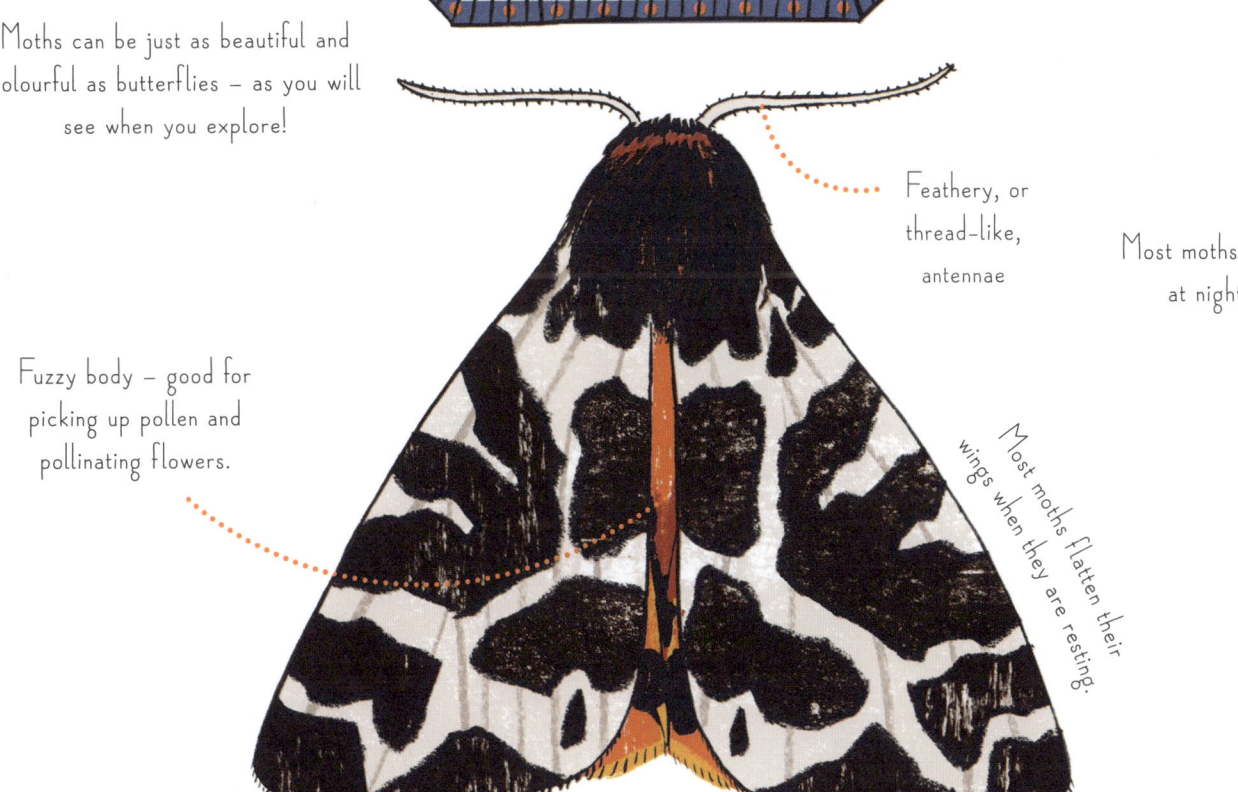

- Feathery, or thread-like, antennae
- Most moths are active at night-time.
- Fuzzy body – good for picking up pollen and pollinating flowers.
- Most moths flatten their wings when they are resting.
- Wings hooked together

BRUSH-FOOTED BUTTERFLIES

Nymphalidae

Meet the brush-footed butterfly family! It is the largest, with over 6,000 species worldwide.

Here you will see some of the most well-known species, such as the monarch, red admiral and painted lady. The front legs of this family are very small and useless for walking. The brush-like front legs of the males give the family its name.

Some butterflies in this family undertake spectacular migrations, the most well-known being the monarch. These golden-orange butterflies escape the cold winters in the US and Canada by flying south in autumn to reach warmer forests in Florida, California and Mexico. They fly north again for the warmer spring and summer months.

Look at the *monarch butterflies* resting in mass on their migration from one part of our house to the other.

GOSSAMER-WINGED BUTTERFLIES

Lycaenidae

Here you will find the gossamer-winged butterflies. They are the second largest butterfly family, containing up to 5,000 species.

This family is made up of the coppers, blues and hairstreaks. Spot these little butterflies by looking at the black and white stripes on their antennae. They often have metallic, shimmering wings and many of the species are very rare. Some of the caterpillars in this family depend on ants for protection from predators. In return for this protection, the caterpillars produce a sugary syrup for the ants to eat as a reward.

Watch the male and female *summer azures* flutter by to land on swamp dogwood flowers. Look for the delicate dusting of soft, blue scales on their wings, before they take to the skies once more.

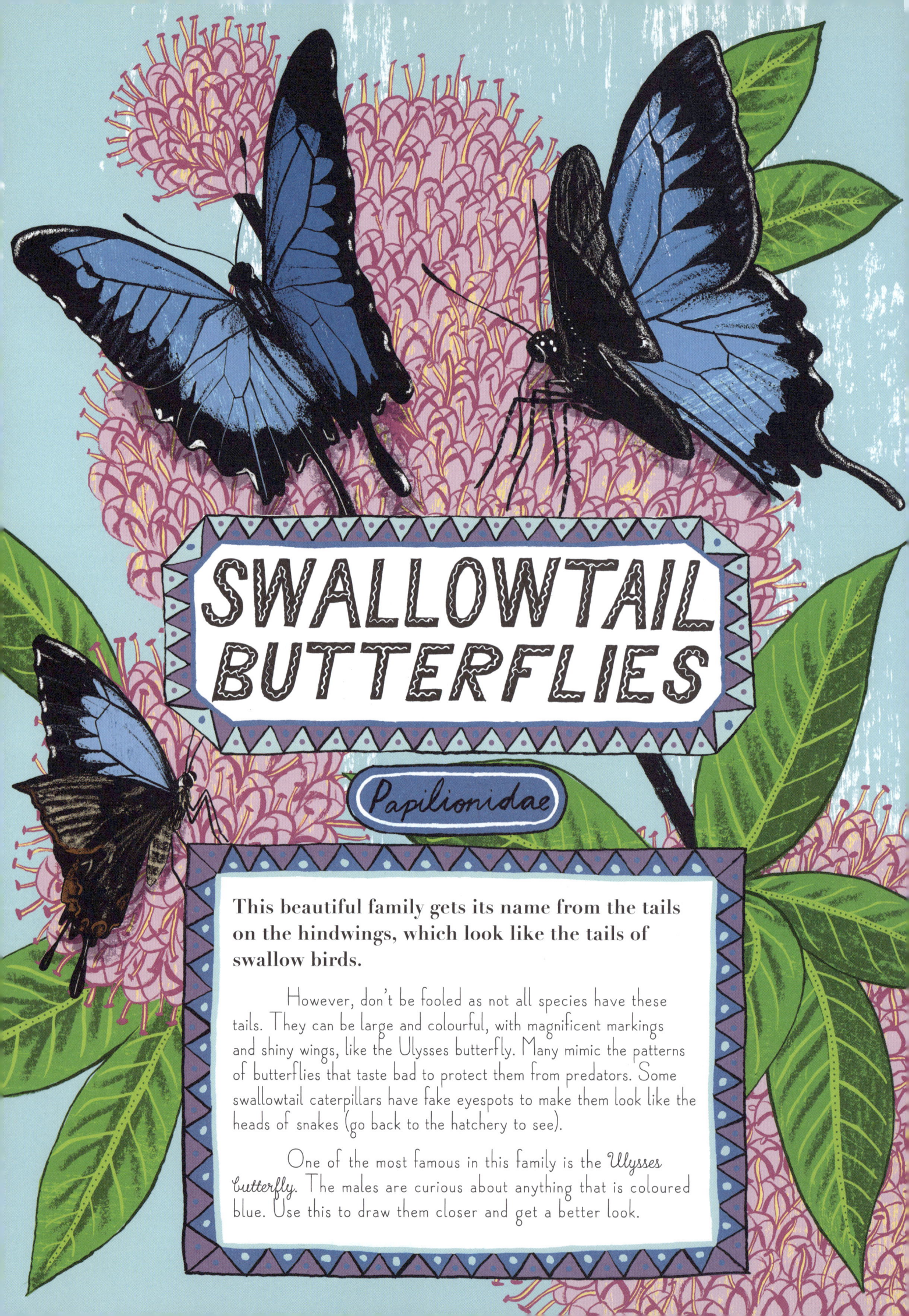

YELLOWS, WHITES, AND SULPHURS

Pieridae

This family gets its name from its colouring. These butterflies don't have the bold patterns of some other families, but they are often beautiful yellow and orange colours, marked with a few black spots.

There are over 1,100 species all over the world, but they are mainly found in Africa and Asia. They can often be seen gathered around water sources. It is thought that the name 'butterfly' came from a species in this family – where an early naturalist called it a 'butter-coloured fly'.

The males of this family often like to visit wet soil to suck up all the salts they need. Look closely at the ground to see some male *sleepy oranges* mud-puddling.

METALMARKS

Riodinidae

The metalmark butterflies get their name from the small metallic spots often found on their wings.

There are more than 1,000 species of metalmark butterflies. Most members of the family can be found in South America, but others live in the tropical areas of Asia and Africa. In general, these butterflies are small in size. One of the smallest – and fluffiest – is the jewelmark butterfly, which is the size of a fingertip. It flies in a rapid and zig-zag way, before landing on its fuzzy legs. Some species have distinctive eyespots on their forewings, like the Loruhama eyemark butterfly. These eyespots can scare off potential predators.

Look at the *rainbow metalmarks* catching sunlight on their metallic wings. How many colours can you see shimmering?

SKIPPERS

Hesperiidae

There are 3,500 species in this family, which are moth-like in their appearance. Many fly during daytime but others fly at dusk.

Skippers have antennae that curve backwards, like a crochet hook. Their eyes are often larger than those of other moths and butterflies, and they have plumper bodies, which are hairy. Their wings are normally smaller in comparison to their bodies, and they may fold their front and back wings over their bodies at slightly different angles. Skippers are named after their flying style — they dart from place to place.

Look at the *large chequered skippers* resting on these long, green leaves. Then, turn the page to visit the moths.

TIGER MOTHS

Arctiinae

There are over 11,000 species in this family, which often have striking geometric markings in orange, black and white, like a tiger.

Many tiger moths have caterpillars with fuzzy bodies, which is why they are often known as 'woolly bears'. But be warned, don't pick them up as the hairs will irritate your skin.

Look at the *garden tiger moths* and caterpillars resting on this foxglove plant. The caterpillars eat its leaves, which makes them poisonous to predators. The adult moth's brightly-patterned wings warn predators that it shouldn't be eaten.

GEOMETER MOTHS

Geometridae

The geometer moths are a very large family of moths, with around 23,000 species named so far.

Many geometer moths have thin abdomens and broad wings, which make them look a lot like butterflies. These moths can be experts in camouflage. The wavy patterns and shapes on their wings often blend into the background. One species in particular is very special: the peppered moth. These little moths' adaptation to their environment is a famous example of Darwin's theory of evolution by natural selection. The pale moths gradually became darker to camouflage against sooty trees in the city. This helped protect them from predators. In the countryside, pale moths thrived because they were camouflaged against clean, pale trees.

See if you can spot both forms of *peppered moth* on the tree bark in the butterfly house.

Caterpillars of geometer moths move in a looping fashion because they do not have legs in the middle of their bodies.

Wavy patterns

1. Latticed heath moth
2. Purple thorn moth
3. Smoky wave moth
4. Small scallop moth
5. Large emerald moth
6. Vestal moth
7. Common pink-barred moth
8. Looper caterpillar
9. Peppered moth (the light form)
10. Peppered moth (the dark form)

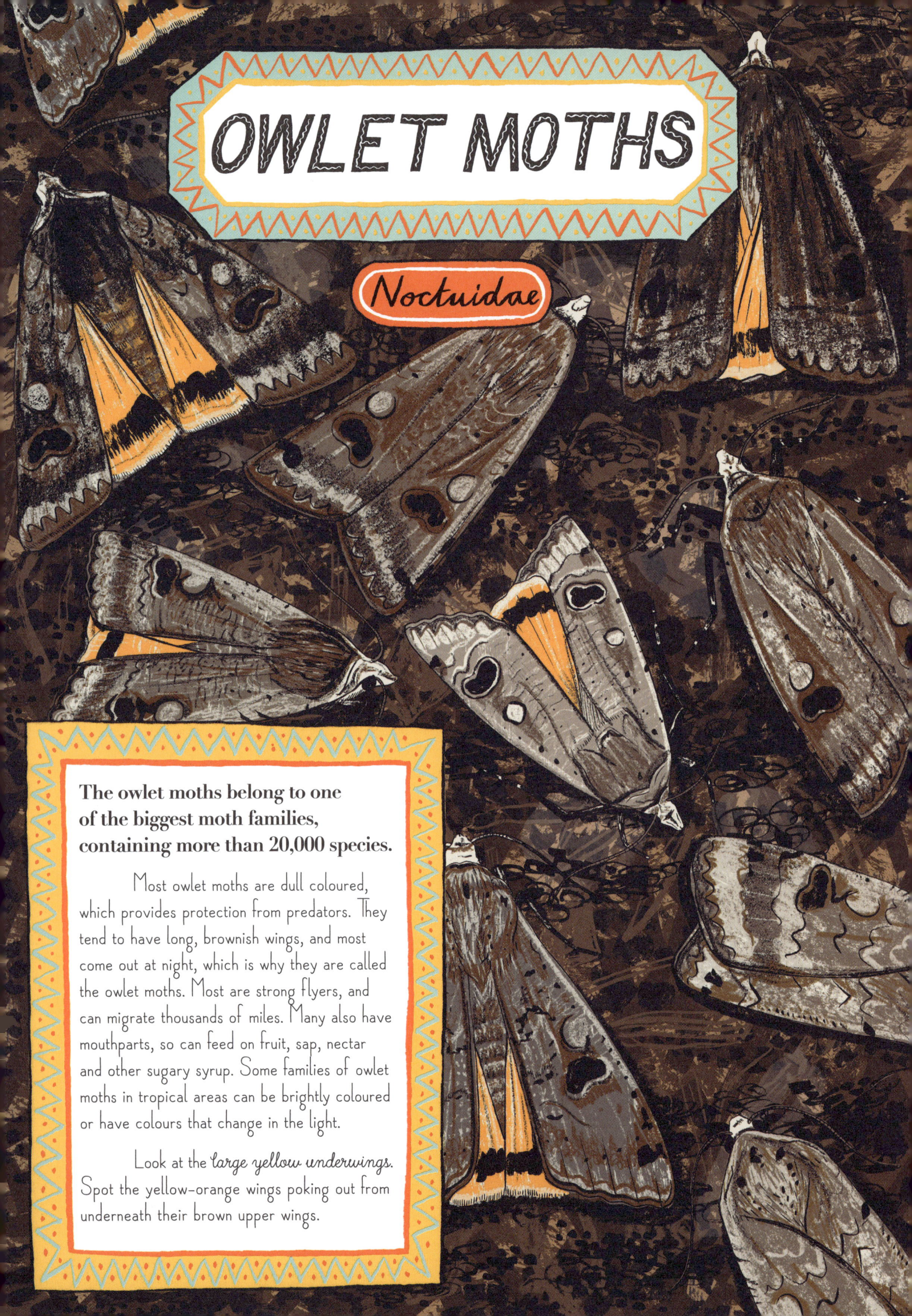

OWLET MOTHS

Noctuidae

The owlet moths belong to one of the biggest moth families, containing more than 20,000 species.

Most owlet moths are dull coloured, which provides protection from predators. They tend to have long, brownish wings, and most come out at night, which is why they are called the owlet moths. Most are strong flyers, and can migrate thousands of miles. Many also have mouthparts, so can feed on fruit, sap, nectar and other sugary syrup. Some families of owlet moths in tropical areas can be brightly coloured or have colours that change in the light.

Look at the *large yellow underwings*. Spot the yellow-orange wings poking out from underneath their brown upper wings.

HAWK MOTHS

Sphingidae

Hawk moths and sphinx moths are fast fliers and beat their wings very quickly. They are found all over the world, but mostly in the tropics.

With their bullet-shaped bodies and narrow, pointed wings, hawk moths are known for their ability to hover, like hummingbirds. A lot of species are also known for pollinating flowers, like orchids and petunias, while they suck up the plant's sugary nectar. Although, the death's head hawk moth steals honey from bees!

Look at the *hummingbird hawk moths* sucking up nectar with their long, hollow tongues. These moths look so similar to hummingbirds that many people think that the actual birds are in their garden.

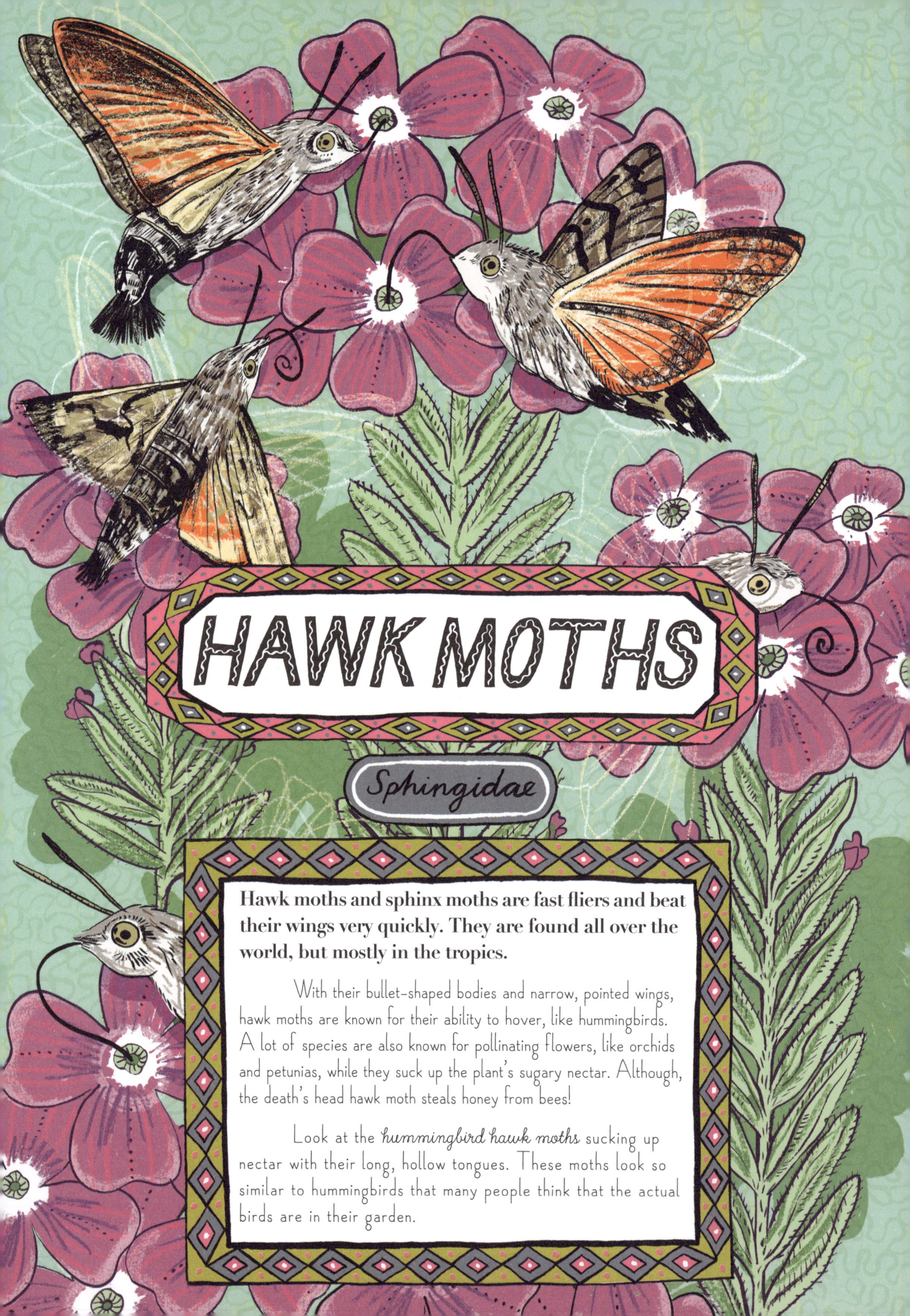

SATURNIID MOTHS

Saturniidae

These moths are also known as the giant silkworm moths. There are about 1,500 species in this family, and they contain some of the largest – and most spectacular – moths in the world.

Many of these moths have large wings, which are brightly coloured – often with eyespots. The largest moth in the family is the atlas moth, with a wingspan of 30cm. The smallest is the rosy maple moth, at under 4cm. Some of these moths produce soft, silken cocoons (pupa).

As night-time draws in at the butterfly house, the *luna moths* start to emerge from hidden cracks and crevices. Look out for their glowing pale-green wings, long tails and eyespot markings.

1. Dark grey fishia moth (Owlet moths); 2. Poplar hawk moth (Hawk moths); 3. Giant leopard moth (Tiger moths); 4. Summer azure butterfly (Gossamer-winged butterflies); 5. Banded king shoemaker (Brush-footed butterflies); 6. Purple spotted swallowtail (Swallowtail butterflies); 7. Rosy maple moth (Saturniid moths); 8. Joseph's coat moth (Owlet moths); 9. Smoky wave moth (Geometer moths); 10. Scarlet tip butterfly (Yellows, whites & sulphurs); 11. Imperial moth (Saturniid moths); 12. Apollo butterfly (Swallowtail butterflies); 13. Common windmill butterfly (Swallowtail butterflies); 14. Indonesian white (Yellow, whites & sulphurs); 15. Eastern tailed blue butterfly (Gossamer-winged butterflies); 16. Small scallop moth (Geometer moths); 17. Common blue butterfly (Gossamer-winged butterflies); 18. Rainbow metalmark (Metalmarks); 19. Obi Island birdwing (Swallowtail butterflies); 20. Red lacewing butterfly (Brush-footed butterflies).